DAWN OF THE HEAVENS AND EARTH

From the Mother of Civilizations, the Father of Prophets Born

Ahod Saleh

Dawn of the heavens and earth

بسم الله الرحمن الرحيم

ثُمَّ أَوْحَيْنَا إِلَيْكَ أَنِ اتَّبِعْ مِلَّةَ إِبْرَاهِيمَ حَنِيفًا ۖ وَمَا كَانَ مِنَ الْمُشْرِكِينَ

﴿١٢٣﴾(النحل)

Then We inspired you: "Follow the faith of Abraham, a Monotheist. And he was not of the polytheists."

(The Qur'an, 16:123)

Research Question

Babylonian men a friend of God and the father of the prophets? How did Babylon outlive the earth? Why is it connected to the modern age?

Abstract

I was part of the modern era. The planet here is suffering; worshipers think of liberalism and do not know its truth; worshipers think of reform; they kill innocent people, animals, and trees. I am from the land of the Arabs, specifically from the Middle East, where people think that customs and traditions are sacred, there are many wars, and they think that they are Muslims, but they are not following true Islam. A great journey, a divine gift, to emerge from the darkness and into the light of knowledge.The way to know the one God.

Introduction

We explained everything in detail.

(The Qur'an, 17:12)

To be and grow up in a century with many wonders about the right way while seeing the billions of humans walk in one direction. Born in an era of time, its people consider themselves part of the age of Modernity that is not valued on Earth as they were able to. In the Modern age, people believe that the empowerment of their technologies conquered the globe. Although humans in that era were one nation, specialized differentiated them from other entities for one reason, they were under the speed of time and fascinated with each other. People at that age followed the policy of grievous error and being under domination. They thought that they were free. However, they are controlled under the theory of divide to conquer. They consider national identity the most significant reason for self-defense, and they ignore the reason for exacting is to research God through the earth is a mystery and to ideology reclamation. This research is written for the upcoming generation from different centuries on the planet. Humans die while books and words stay to guide humanity.

The modern century was named because of the empowerment of Metal iron. It is the Comprehensive era, marked in part by technological innovations, urbanization, scientific discoveries, and globalization. The Modern Age is generally split into two parts: the early and the late modern period. The Modern Age is generally split into two parts: the early and the late modern periods. (METADATA, March 22, 2016).

Under the ideology of Modernity, the Superpower in the contemporary age covered their corruption on earth. They caused wars and were born from the struggle and suffering of humans. The concept of state is to make an iron border between the land to spread their domination and continue the Superpower U.S.A. made the American Continent as the nation and the other continents and lands a small state. Such as the mother and her children. There have always been certain beliefs that everything on earth is detailed by the Lord and sent to humans through the Prophets to put the earth's new system for humans. Also, some people have been able to reach sciences and progress on the ground more than people have achieved in the modern era, but when I searched for the Babylonians, I found the answers.

Abraham *peace be upon him:* Babylonian Abraham bin Terah bin Nahor bin Argo bin Falekh bin Aber bin Shalekh bin Arfakhshad bin Sam bin Norouh bin Lamek bin Mutushlakh bin Hanuj bin Yared bin Mahlayel bin Qain bin Anoush bin Sheth bin Adam. (Mohammad, 2022)

THIESS STATEMENT

Verily We have honored the children of Adam. We carry them on land and sea, have provided good things for them, and have preferred them above many of those whom We created with a marked preferment

(The Qur'an, 15:70)

It has always been assumed that God created the universe from nothing and humans from a single soul. This is what needs to be fixed in humans. However, depending on the century in which a person lives, it changes how he adapts to life. Modernity is not as important as it is sometimes claimed. For example, great achievements in the religious realm were made without modernity, and modernity itself is not a reason for the corruption of the modern era. This planet has been walked on by people who have outlived the earth since the beginning of humanity. From the Babylonian age, when Uruk III, the Early Dynastic, sent Abraham, peace be upon him, in 2000 BC, to the final messenger, Prophet Mohammad, peace be upon him, in the 7th century CE, that reshaped the earth's systems until the planet's end.

Nature of Religion

Earth, in the language, is the planted that the science of gravity has flattened for creators to live on Earth indefinitely. So set thou thy face steadily and truly to the Faith: (establish) Allah's handiwork according to the pattern on which He has made mankind: no change (let there be) in the work (wrought) by Allah; that is the standard Religion, but most among mankind understand not. (The Qur'an,21:30)God created the world billions of years ago, and another creator has walked into Earth on this planet. The beginning of the new dawn is that God wants to create an unknown creator on Earth. According to the Quran, "And (remember) when your Lord said to the angels: "Verily, I am going to place (mankind) generations after generations on earth." They said: "Will You place therein those who will make mischief therein and shed blood, - while we glorify You with praises and thanks (Exalted be You above all that they associate with You as partners) and sanctify You." He (Allah) said: "I know that which you do not know" (QURAN, 2022) God should prepare the Earth for the new excluded creation by creating other creations. Their process and reason in life are to declare his glory and subdue them to serve the human needs and purpose from existence. According to the Holy book Quran, "The seven heavens and the

Earth, and all beings therein, declare His glory: there is not a thing but celebrates His praise; And yet ye understand not how they declare His glory! Verily He is Oft-Forbear, Most Forgiving! (Lord) . God is written in the destiny of humans, "God Slaves," from their faith, life, livelihood, names, color, gender, date of birth, and death.

On the other hand, Temple liturgies were primarily directed toward the 'care and feeding of the gods.'37 To what extent temples catered to the spit-ritual needs of human beings is much more difficult to determine. Individuals could make donations - from humble offerings to enslaved people and valuable cult furniture - which constituted gifts to the deities - to 'make their hearts glow.' The protagonist of the Babylon poem Indlal bel nemesis ('I will praise the Lord of Wisdom), who like the Biblical Job, is inflicted with a variety of physical and mental suffering, turns to the temple of Marduk, the Esagila' with prostration and supplication' and performs various devotions at the different gates of the temple". (Leick, 2003) destiny was different for the Babylonians. They believed that those who are destinated in their actions are the plants, stars, sun, moon, and the Ancient. The Babylonian faith is in nature and universal. Who created character and the secrets of the Universe? By the Originator in creation. The heritage of Ancient Babylon civilization is that for each of the Earth's nature there was a God to worship by human-made"(Liltambir-Shamash). Women usually bore names referring to goddesses. The study of people's names can contemplate much of the relative popularity of deities in a place and period.

"Possessing powers greater than that of humans, many gods were associated with celestial phenomena such as the sun, moon, and stars, others with the forces of nature such as winds and fresh and ocean waters, yet others with real animals—lions, bulls, wild oxen—and imagined creatures such as fire-spitting dragons. In the Sumerian hymn "Enlil in the E-Kur," the god Enlil is described as controlling and animating nature." (Spar, April 2009) Faithfully, those Ancients are their gods. They want to empty their religion of anthropology, make an Ancient, and discriminate them from other Ancient to consolidate their civilization. Because of their blind beliefs, they want to keep their gods to worship for the next generations through the centuries. Historically, archaeologists studied to solve the mysteries and puzzles of their faith in statuses through their Ancients. Furthermore, they were sanctified of their gods that their heritage through their Ancient they specialized the gods in a significant color of eyes and shape.

Although, through Anthropology, human nature is one, its interact and impact the cultures, type of body shapes, tongues, colors, and environment throughout the century. The fixed divine order in creatures is the spiritual nature. However, it differentiates by the human path of faith. They want to believe in monotheism or worship a universe, gnomes, or traps. According to the Anthropological Origins of "Culture," The culture of an organization eminently influences its myriad decisions and actions. A company's prevailing ideas, values, attitudes, and beliefs guide how its employees think, feel, and act—quite often unconsciously. Therefore, understanding culture is fundamental to describing and analyzing organizational phenomena. For some, culture is considered the "glue" that holds an organization together, and for others, the "compass" that provides direction. (Taylor, 2014)

Certainly, of a discrepancy between the father of prophets Abraham, peace be upon him is people of the Babylonians, and the age of Modernism, the culture of modern humans, is similar and had not improved through the centuries in some lands from the factor of idols. However, it is different from the method of making idols. A few years ago, I went to Thailand, especially the capital of Bangkok, the current modern age. I saw a big fetish made of Iron brass incarnate while the human gathered into it; they prayed, put flowers, cried, and prostration. At that moment surprising effects, the idol does not respond to them. Who creates the iron that is the idol made from?! There is an immense power that is detailed and will create other creatures, while this idol is a creature from the creator. The science of religion shows, "the extant versions of the complete life of the Buddha were composed four hundred or more years after his death. Drawing on much earlier material from the canonical Sutras (Discourses) and Vinaya (Discipline); they fill in the gaps in the canonical accounts with a fabric of myth (which many Buddhists be-lieve to be true) and literary invention. The authors viewed the Buddha as an epic hero, and their purpose was to celebrate his deeds. They were not histo- rians but poets and propagandists. For instance, Asvagho~a (first century C.E.), in his epic Buddhacarita (Acts ofthe Buddha), depicted Gautama as a genuine human being; his narrative, even where it may not be historical, is dramati- cally authentic. The hero is a mortal experiencing conflicts; undergoing gen- uine temptations; trying, and ultimately rejecting, false courses; exercising choice at every point; and prevailing, not through fate or divine intervention, but through his own action. He is motivated by compassion for suffering hu- manity and exhibits the martial virtues of courage, steadfastness, initiative, and self-discipline. Throughout his ordeals he sustains a delicate sensitivity and an unshakable dignity" (JOHNSON, 1997)

How similar is this attractive of idols from the second era of human beings in 1595 BC? The Babylonians had made a human figure. Also, the Babylonians believed Mardukh had a family characterized by wives and children from other civilizations from another land. The historians indicate, Babylonians viewed the god Marduk as the ultimate supreme being and made him their national god. "A Babylonian myth about how the world was created details Marduk's rise as the chief god. Known as the Epic of Creation, the story was written on seven clay tablets and publicly recited in Babylon annually on the fourth day of the New Year festival. It described the ceremony at which Marduk was appointed to his high position in this way":

'Of the outer walls of the temples were decorated with attractive the great gods all of them who determines destinies... filled the Hall of Assembly.... They embraced each other... they held conversation... they ate bread, they drank wine. they were carefree.... For Marduk, their avenger... they set him on a princely throne [and proclaimed] "You are the most honored one among the great gods, your decree is law. From this very day your command shall be unalterable.... No one among the gods shall overstep your bounds. . . . We have' (LANDAU, 1997)

When God sent to the friend prophet Abraham, peace be upon him. The prophet started to argue and preaches about Monotheistic Hanifism. According to the last heavenly book, 'Quran' Allah 'God tells about the arguments that Allah gave his prophet Abraham the argumentive wisdom to approve the Babylonians on their wrong path and believes in their village. (51) And We had certainly given Abraham his sound judgement before,[891] and We were of him well-Knowing (52) When he said to his father and his people, "What are these statues to which you are devoted?" (53) They said, "We found our fathers worshippers of them. (54) He said, "You were certainly, you and your fathers, in manifest error." (55) They said, "Have you come to us with truth, or are you of those who jest?" (56) He said, "[No], rather, your Lord is the Lord of the heavens and the earth who created them, and I, to that, am of those who testify. (The prophets I Chapter 17 Verse 51-56)

My attempt there is human nature is one. However, its influenced by the age that humanity is part of. There are pure similarities between the Buddhists in modernism and the Babylonians. The differences are in the culture, type of idols, and century. There is a similarity between the god of Buddhists 'Nirvana' and the gods of Mrdduk, who are an idol made of iron, and They cannot speak, listen, benefit, or harm. However, it is differentiated by myths. Therefore, clay and clay have the following whims because, by nature, human is a voluntary creature. The fatal sin is the arrogance of some modern 'civilized' humans because it lets blind insight to even that their vanity does not allow them to search for the truth, which guides more corruption that affects other generations and centuries. Through the last heavenly book, Allah approved that the argumentive ways should be by the selected person who can argue the humans by maturity and portent because Allah honored the human brain more than other creatures.

Human Knowledge

When did most people stop searching for science, right, and research on the earth's planet? The answer is that they thought they were stronger than them and constated the world with their small discoveries. Through modernity, knowledge had renamed to the education factor. They built construction industries to educate people about the earth and human existence, improving the quality of life. However, the type of knowledge had been dying at that period. There is one fact that caused many different results. It is the way of 'cooptation temptation of corruption Branches from it. Examples are bribery, moneylending, money laundering, and the hegemony of a unipolar economic capital system. The studies indicate, ', *corruption is caused by the selfish nature of people exhibited through excessive and misguided government regulations as well as the government participation in the economy. The most common form of corruption is "conflict of interests," where politicians and/or public administrators engage in private dealings with the government-directly or indirectly-and charge inflated rates for govern- ment contracts, in a sense siphoning money out of the public treasury. The level of corruption existent within a system is determined by the national culture, the overall quality of the political system, the institutions that are entrusted to fight corruption, the quality of the democratic system, the political party system, the public adminis- trative system, and the level of decentralization. The obvious problem in attempting to analyze corruption is the limited and the unreliable nature of the data, therefore the instrument chosen to study corruption is of utmost importance. The traditional instruments utilized in evaluating national levels of corruption are: The International Country Risk Guide'* (Văduva, 2016)

Why did humans need a system the creator chose to have a better life on earth? Like the Babylonians, they had corruption in their territories resulting from the pagan community. Through the archaeologists, *"AMOUS BABYLONIAN LEADERS HAMMURABI Babylonian king from 1792 to 1750 B.C Expanded the city-state of Babylon along the Euphrates River to unite all of southern Mesopotamia His code, a collection of 282 laws and standards, stipulated rules for commercial interactions and set fines and punishments to meet the requirements of justice. He ordered these laws recorded on a slab of stone that measured 8 feet high and copied on stone tablets so they could be disseminated to the provinces ruled by the Babylonian empire. These laws were retributive in nature"* (B.C.E.), n.d.) *The roles represented,*

- This code recognized that kingly power derived from God and that earthly rulers had moral duties, as did their subjects. It laid out Hammurabi's task "to bring about the rule of righteousness in the land, to destroy the wicked and the evil-doers" and to fear God.
- Hammurabi ordered these laws recorded in a slab of stone which measure eight feet high, copied on clay tablets so they can be disseminated to the provinces ruled by the Babylonian Empire.

- These laws were retributive in nature. It means "an eye for an eye, a tooth for a tooth." Punishments were meted out based on the gravity of the offense.
- As the rule of conduct was binding on all members of the community, state, and nation, the code provided coherent boundaries for citizens in a complex society.
- Citizens understood that abiding by these rules meant freedom to live and prosper.
- Although punishments for many minor infractions appear draconian by contemporary standards, the code formalized the fundamental responsibility of the individual to act in the context of the public interest.
- The code was grounded in commonly accepted principles of morality and ethics and provided a clear set of norms for all members of society to live together in peace.

I can return to the critical crossroad. Why did human needs to have a system that the creator of them chose to have a better life on earth? A similar through the Babylonians was corruption spread by the Babylonians. An Example of moral depravity is, Making the system of the god pagan has several reasons. Still, the most important of them—is a matter of their worldly desires and satisfying the human instinct of religion. The spread of corruption begins in man through his faith and what it commands him to do. Among their pleasures are their desires, trade, self-pleasure, a corrupt economic system that makes sculptures and sells them as gods, human trafficking, and dealing with biodiversity with a pagan system that leads to the destruction of the earth, the animals. Did paganism create anything?

So how do you deal with someone who doesn't exist anywhere else? That is why Allah sent the human prophets to warn, missionaries, and holy books full of enormous systems, roles, and ethics; the primary purpose of human approaches is because the earth is a place where devils and sins. The Quran explains the reason of sent the prophets,"And We send not the Messengers except as giver of glad tidings and warners. But those who disbelieve, dispute with false argument, in order to refute the truth thereby. And they treat My Ayat (proofs, evidences, verses, lessons, signs, revelations, etc.), and that with which they are warned, as jest and mockery"!(The Cave, Chapter 15 , verse 56). The substantial value of spiritual relations is that benefits human. According to psychologists, several specific character strengths in the VIA classification are embedded in the sacred literature of the world's major religious traditions. For example, concepts of forgiveness are mentioned 234 times in the Qur'an (Rye et al., 2000). Moreover, theologians, religious leaders, and scientists in the broader field of spirituality would agree that many character strengths in the VIA classification are "spiritual" in nature. These include, but are not limited to, the character strengths of humility, gratitude, forgiveness, awe (appreciation of beauty), kindness, hope, fairness, and love. (Psychol., 2020 Aug 14.)

On the other hand, lately, the people start look at the relationships between Allah and his slave is confined polytheism or disbelief because of many reasons. An Example, people used the concept and ideology of religious people to get the religion role while they forgot those people who is toke the religion and Allah is books are human has a virtues and disadvantages. Those people used their position and collaborated with Satan 'evil path' they distorted the heavenly books make it Irregular with the human mind, it is of no use to man. For the benefit of these people in the world's political influence, Satan made a more significant number of people in hell, seducing the servants and grand corruption in the land. Therefore, the distortion made divisions the community into parties and groups. An example is religiously, politically, economically, and militarily, that is negatively impacts the land systems. Although, Allah sent last messenger prophet Mohammad peace be upon him he is from descendants of prophets Abraham peace be upon him and his religion as all prophets does. Islam by the last heavenly books Quran in protected from the misrepresenting, the majority of Muslims people through the modern century are following the religious people who are seductive and mislead the Islam Sharia to political interests that cased damages, terrorism, and corruption into the Islamic world resulted by the sects and civil wars under of the misguided imams. According to the Prophet Mohammad peace be upon him is speech '*Abu Dhar said, "I was with the Prophet ﷺ one day and I heard him saing: "There is something I fear for my Ummah than the Dajjal. It was then that I became afraid, so I said: 'Oh Rasool Allah! Which thing is that?" He ﷺ said, "Misguided and astray scholars."* (Sunan Tirmizi, 2013-2022)

Literature in Language

Through the Prophet Abraham peace be upon him, peoples the Babylonians knew of communication of Allah 'God' is revelations vow by tongue his people. The Babylonians used their emotional explanation of their idols Babylonians used their literature too. The Babylonians also used their literature. Such as literature, poetry, writing, and sculpture, as a source to worship the idols. Allah creates them and excites their language to explain their needs, communicate with each other, and detail some language sustenance to be worthy of worship reason humans on the earth. Babylonian also used their literature to explanation about their status to the gods of Ancient. An Example the poetry. According to the literary historians. "Without the Great Mountain Enlil . . . the carp would not . . . come straight up from the sea, they would not dart about. The sea would not produce all its heavy treasure, no freshwater fish would lay eggs in the reedbeds, no bird of the sky would build nests in the spacious lands; in the sky, the thick clouds would not open their mouths; on the fields, dappled grain would not fill the arable lands, vegetation would not grow lushly on the plain; in the gardens, the spreading trees of the mountain would not yield fruit". (Spar I. , April 2009). People in modernity, on the other hand, do not prioritize literature. It has the academic sector; it just uses it in educational, governmental, and subjectable small books and newspapers because people are interested in platforms and social media.

Astronomy/Astrology

What is the reason that is resulted to discover the space? who is discover it and through what? Sumerians and Babylonian discovered space is for their gods and idols. Although they did not search for who created the universe and humans, they used their idols as a reason. According to the archaeologists, En Henduanna is the earliest female known to have had a connection with astronomy. She was the daughter of Sargon of Akkad who established the Sargonian Dynasty in Babylon. He appointed her the chief priestess of the moon goddess of the city – a position of great power and prestige. Only through the auspices of the high priestess could a leader achieve a legitimate claim to rule. Of her written work, translations of 48 of her poems survive. To put her in perspective, astronomy began with the priests and priestesses in Sumeria and Babylon. As early as 3000 BC, these sacred temples in Sumer were complex structures that directed every essential activity of life including trade, farming, and crafts. The priests and priestesses established a network of observatories to monitor the movements of the stars. The calendar they created is still used to date certain religious events like Easter and Passover". (daviddarling, 2016)

As the Babylonians learned the sciences of the universe and worshiped the stars and planets, Allah sent Prophet Abraham to them to confirm Allah's oneness by reflecting the stars and creating the stars. After a thousand decades, the last prophet was not too certain. but for the entire world. Who are Abraham's offspring through his son Esmail. May peace be upon him. The Quran is Allah's final testament. May peace be upon Muhammad, the last human prophet. The Quran has a piece of specific information about the number of skies and the types of creatures in the universe. Muslims began several sciences and discoveries that benefit humans and play an important role in modern development as a result of the Quran. Throughout the centuries, Muslims have relied on the Quran and Al-Hadith as primary sources for discovery, science, and research into a wide range of topics. Therefore, the universe is an

In the same way, people discover space and begin the human journey into space through the technological century enabled by Allah's permission. Allah awoke the soul of a prophet named Mohammad after he finished the Islam religion and the Quran. "This day I have perfected your religion for you and completed My favor to you. I have approved Islam to be your religion. (As for) he who does not intend to commit a sin but is constrained by hunger to eat of what is forbidden, then surely Allah is Forgiving, Merciful." (Quran, AL-MAEDA (THE TABLE) , Sura 5: verse 3). The Islamic civilization began with a new era in history. Muslims began to spread Islam's invitation, discover the last holy book, make scientific discoveries, take on moral roles, and live lives full of dignity and knowledge that is made the mordren life today. According to the historians, "A significant number of inventions were produced by medieval Muslim engineers and inventors, such as Abbas Ibn Firnas, the Banū Mūsā, Taqi al-Din, and most notably al-Jazari.Some of the inventions journalist Paul Vallely has stated to have come from the Islamic Golden Age include the camera obscura, coffee, soap bar, toothpaste, shampoo, distilled alcohol, uric acid, nitric acid, alembic, valve, reciprocating suction piston pump, mechanized water clocks, quilting, surgical catgut, vertical-axle windmill, inoculation, cryptanalysis, frequency analysis, three-course meal, stained glass and quartz glass, Persian carpet, and a celestial globe.The concept of Urbanization, the city of Baghdad was the capital of the Abbasid Leaders and a major center of learning and trade in the world. As urbanization increased, Muslim cities grew unregulated, resulting in narrow winding city streets and neighbourhoods separated by different ethnic backgrounds and religious affiliations. Suburbs lay just outside the walled city, from wealthy residential communities to working-class semi-slums. City garbage dumps were located far from the city, as were clearly defined cemeteries which were often homes for criminals. A place of prayer was found just near one of the main gates, for religious festivals and public executions. Similarly, military training grounds were found near the main gate.Muslim cities also had advanced domestic water systems with sewers, public baths, drinking fountains, piped drinking water supplies, and widespread private and public toilet and bathing facilities.The demographics of medieval Islamic society varied in some significant aspects from other agricultural societies, including a decline in birth rates as well as a change in life expectancy. Other traditional agrarian societies are estimated to have had an average life expectancy of 20 to 25 years, while ancient Rome and medieval Europe are estimated at 20 to 30 years. Conrad I. Lawrence estimates the average lifespan in the early Islamic Caliphate to be above 35 years for the general population, and several studies on the life spans of Islamic scholars concluded that members of this occupational group had a life expectancy between 69 and 75 years, though this longevity was not representative of the general population.The early Islamic civilization also had the highest literacy rates among pre-modern societies, alongside the city of classical Athens in the 4th century BC, and later, China after the introduction of printing from the 10th century. One factor for the relatively high literacy rates in the early Islamic Empire was its parent-driven educational marketplace, as the state did not systematically subsidize educational services until the introduction of state funding under Nizam al-Mulk in the 11th century. Another factor was the diffusion of paper from China, which led to an efflorescence of books and written culture in Islamic society, thus papermaking technology transformed Islamic society (and later, the rest of Afro-Eurasia) from an oralto scribal culture, comparable to the later shifts from scribal to typographic culture, and from typographic culture to the Internet. Other factors include the widespread use of paper books in Islamic society (more so than any other previously existing society), the study and memorization of the Qur'an, flourishing commercial activity, and the emergence of the Maktub and Madrasah educational institutions.In sciences, early scientific methods were developed in the Islamic world, where significant progress in methodology was made, especially in the works of Ibn al-Haytham (Alhazen) in the 11th century, who is considered a pioneer of experimental physics, which someplace in the experimental tradition of Ptolemy. Others see his use of experimentation and quantification to distinguish between competing scientific theories as an innovation in the scientific method. Ibn al-Haytham (Alhazen) wrote the Book of Optics, in which he significantly reformed the field of optics, empirically proved that vision occurred because of light rays entering the eye, and invented the camera obscura to demonstrate the physical nature of light rays (The, 1982)"

In my attempt, the reason for man's existence is God, a truth that cannot be argued with. How can man's progress on earth be without knowing his systems except by following God's books and religion? God will make one book firm for the Day of Judgment if there are any irrational religions. Religion is the main factor that drives the earth. Religion cannot be cornered. How can a person reach space without knowing space? How will he know where to go? God told about it in His books because man is honored with his mind by the all-knowing, all-aware Creator. He knows how to address those who were created.

Occasions and Feats

Prophet Abraham peace be upon him. Argue with his Babylonian people about monotheism ONE LORD "Allah". Babylonians had a discrepancy. Although, they used priests, and clairvoyants to exorcise evil and the spirit of evil to have their eternal ability beyond nature. The archaeologists indicate, "Indeed some scholars suggest that religion was the motivating force behind the transformation from village to city life. The rulers of the region all considered themselves to be agents of the gods and an important part of their duties was the performance of ceremonies designed to ward off evil and gain the deities' goodwill. The principal centers for religious activities were the temples, though in certain cultures ceremonies could. Also, take place in sacred groves or on hilltops. The gods were present in the temples in the form of divine statues, and the priests were responsible for looking after them. There were different types of priests with special functions including administration, incantations, exorcism, omens, divination, and so on. Most of the available information comes from texts dealing with the palace or the temple; little is known about the religion of the ordinary citizen." (Roaf, 1990)

The Babylonians were too knowledgeable and found a role part of the universe because they believed the planets were gods. How did they see the plants? They use it as a resource to know the prescience through the star sites. Islamic historical perspective believes, there was a King named Nimrod astrologers saw from the star sites that there was a man who saw the reason for the end of king Namroids reign. The Quran approved the importance of the star sites," I swear by the fallings of the stars (75) and that is a mighty oath if you but knew. The Quran approved about the importance of the star sites," The Quran approved the importance of the star sites," I swear by the fallings of the stars (75) and that is a mighty oath if you but knew (76)" (AL-WAQIA). The king commanded the army to kill every newborn male in the kingdom of Babylon to protect his position. (AL-WAQIA). The king commanded the army to kill every newborn of males in kingdom of Babylon to protect his position.

Comparable, during modern history. People have shown human nature, however, in different ages and methods. An Example of occasions relates to religious holidays, is Islam, Judaism, Christianity, other believable religion, national, liberation, independency, and marriage.

Miracle Started with the Born of Prophets peace be upon them

How did prophet Abraham bear into an era of a Tyrant king in New Babylon who killed Children in the kingdom?_sometimes the story narratives reflect lessons for those of the first mind for flexible life systems. Through the prophet Abraham s story, the prophecy of miracles started. After a year, the prophet Abraham peace be upon him is born and his mother hid it in a cave to protect him from the killed. The studies show, "The Cave of Abraham,the Birth Place of

Prophet Abraham in Urfa is a famous pilgrimage site where devotees go to pray and pay respects to one of history's most revered prophets.He is believed to have been born in a cave in Urfa where he spent about ten years of his life as protection against the cruel King Nimrod who then ordered all newborn children killed upon learning of Abraham's coming birth.A praying area in the cave was constructed, but the exact spot where Abraham was born is protected by a glass encasement. There are also faucets where devotees wash their hands with holy water.Entrance to the cave is via the same courtyard shared with the Mevlid-I Halil Mosque". (turkeytravelcentre, 2022). From the father of prophets is miracles given by Lord through the Islamic Historians is "The child was alone in the cave with no one to care for him. He was sucking the milk which flowed of his fingers - by the grace of Almighty God. The child grew up under Allah's protection. From time to time, his mother would come secretly to the cave to watch him". (Islamic organsization, 1995-2022)

When the Prophet Abraham Peace was upon him when reached 13. He was brought out from the cave by his mother in the evening. The Abrahamboy saw the sky and said; where is my Lord? They argue and pause in Abraham Peace be upon him, that what let him from the first look at the sky to ask about his religious nature? that explained a very important about Anthropology through civilization anthropology explained. When a human grows without life distractions the first thing that he would ask after mental puberty is the search for the Lord. Is represented by an investigation, of the reason for existence. Prophet AbrahamPeace be upon him stay grows up in a cave only knowing his mother. According to the Quran, "75. Thus We showed Abraham the empire of the heavens and the earth, so that he may be of those with certainty76. When the night fell over him, he saw a planet. He said, "This is my lord!" But when it set, he said, "I do not like those that set. 77. Then, when he saw the moon rising, he said, "This is my lord!" But when it set, he said, "If my Lord does not guide me, I will be of the misguided people." 78. Then, when he saw the sun rising, he said, "This is my Lord!—it is the biggest." But when it set, he said, "O my people, I am innocent of your idolatry. 79. I have turned my attention towards Him Who created the heavens and the earth—a monotheist—and I am not of the polytheists." (Livestock, Chapter 8 Verse 75 until 79).

The seondery miracle of the father of Prophets Abraham Peace be upon him. Related to the Quran, the Bablyianon argued Abraham about his faith in Allah as a montheist , invtiation to A monthesim the. "And We gave Abraham his sound judgment formerly, and We knew him well" (The Prophets Chapter 17). So, he got the argument, wisdom, and ingenuity from Lord "Allah" to be able to argue with the Babylonians about convincing arguments to repel them from idolatry to monotheism.

Roots of Israel

Was the prophet Abraham's father the father of the Israelites? The studies indicate, "Abraham, Hebrew Avraham, originally called Abram or, in Hebrew, Avram, (flourished early 2nd millennium BCE), the first of the Hebrew patriarchs and a figure revered by the three great monotheistic religions—Judaism, Christianity, and Islam. According to the biblical book of Genesis, Abraham left Ur, in Mesopotamia, because God called him to found a new nation in an undesignated land that he later learned was Canaan. He obeyed unquestioningly the commands of God, from whom he received repeated promises and a covenant that his "seed" would inherit the land. In Judaism the promised offspring is understood to be the

Jewish people descended from Abraham's son, Isaac, born of his wife Sarah. Similarly, in Christianity the genealogy of Jesus is traced to Isaac, and Abraham's near-sacrifice of Isaac is seen as a foreshadowing of Jesus' sacrifice on the cross. In Islam it is Ishmael, Abraham's firstborn son, born of Hagar, who is viewed as the fulfillment of God's promise, and the Prophet Muhammad is his descendant. (Parrot, 2022)

The main argument, after World War II, many Jews immigrated to Palestine to establish a state in the modern concept of the Jews. Given that they see the Al-Aqsa Mosque as belonging to the Children of Israel because they are the descendants of Jacob, son of Isaac, son of Abraham, may God bless him and grant him peace. But in fact, immigration was not religious but rather a political reason for the establishment of the Zionist entity, which serves the interests of Britain and America in the Arab region. This region thrived for nearly a thousand years. Then came a great flood called colonialism. It is indeed the territory of religions and prophets, but it is not the home of the Jews in the modern world. There has been an occupied country from 1948 to this year, 2022. It is called Palestine. The Palestinians suffer from the most severe types of racial discrimination: displacement, killing, and diaspora. Because of the occupation, Israel existed not to establish a Jewish state but to destabilize the security of the Arab region so that America's hegemony would continue. There is Mecca, a sacred place for all Muslims. Why don't all Muslims congregate in Saudi Arabia under the banner of Mecca to establish a Muslim state?They are certain from their preserved holy book that Mecca and Medina are sacred places to which a Muslim must come to perform the laws of Islam and then return to his country. Why do not the Jews implement this system in Al-Aqsa Mosque? Because the Europeans do not want their Jews because they view them as hard-line and against the liberalism of the West's progress, they put forward that argument. In addition to convincing the people of this, they created the concept of terrorism—Islamic extremism—that serves the domination of the West and claims death for America and Israel because of its corruption in the moral and religious systems. It is at their mercy. Islam is innocent of spoilers.

Conclusion

To conclude, it has always been important to work on this research, which shows the importance of religion, the reason for existence, the prophets, peace be upon him, differences, conflicts on land, succession in land, the value of life, when it loses its value it becomes a place for corruption, because it loses the main factor of existence, which is faith in God.

Bibliography

Al-Isra / verse70. (2019). quran4all.ne.

AL-WAQIA, Q. (n.d.). *Chapter 27: Verse 75 & 76.* AL-WAQIA .

B.C.E.), w. (.-1. (n.d.). *BABYLONIAN EMPIRE (circa 1790 - 1595 B.C.E.).* Retrieved from weebly.com.

daviddarling. (2016). *1.* Retrieved from daviddarling.info.

Islamic organsization. (1995-2022). Prophet Ibrahim and the Idol Worship. *Al-Islam*, 1.

JOHNSON, W. L. (1997). 1.3 THE BIOGRAPHY OF THE BUDDH. In S. A. Wawrytko, *The Buddhist Religion A Historical Introduction* (p. 29). University of Wisconsin: Wadsworth Publishing Company.

LANDAU, E. (1997). *The Babylonians.* Inistitute of the Uneversity of Chicago : Millfors Road .

Leick, G. (2003). *The Bablonians an Intorduction* . London and New York: Taylor and Florence Production Ltd .

Livestock. (Chapter 8 Verse 75 until 79).

Livestock. (n.d.). Chapter 8 Verse from 75 until 79.

Lord. (n.d.). *44 Al-Isra* . alro7.net.

METADATA. (March 22, 2016). *Understanding the media and Culture* . U.S.A, Minnesota : Uneversity of Minnesota Driven Discover,LIBRARIES,.

Mohammad, S. A. (2022). What is the linage of Abraham? *answers.mawdoo3*, 1.

Parrot, A. (2022, October 18). *britannica.* Retrieved from 1.

Psychol., F. (2020 Aug 14.). The Relationship Between Spirituality, Health-Related Behavior, and Psychological Well-Being. *NIH NLM Logo*, 1.

Quran. (n.d.). *AL-MAEDA (THE TABLE) , Sura 5: verse 3 .*

Quran. (n.d.). Al-room.

Quran. (n.d.). *The CattleI |165 verses | Chapter 7.*

QURAN, H. B. (2022). *Al-baqraa/ verse 30 Chapter 1.* https://surahquran.org/.

Roaf, M. (1990). *Cultutre Atlas of Mesopotmaia and the Ancient Near East* . Printed in Spain: Brian Vikander / CORBIS.

Spar, I. (April 2009). HEILBRUNN TIMELINE OF ART HISTORY ESSAYS Mesopotamian Deities. *TheMetmuseum*, 1.

Spar, I. (April 2009). Mesopotamian Deities. *Metmuseum orgnization* , 1.

Sunan Tirmizi, K. a. (2013-2022). *Misguided And Stray Scholars* . Iraq: qrakitab.com/p/misguided-and-stray-scholars.html.

T. G. (1982 , May/June). *his article appeared on pages 6-13* . Retrieved from islamichistory.org/: print edition of Saudi Aramco World.

Taylor, J. (2014). *Organizational Culture and the Paradox of Performance Management.* www.academia.edu/.

The Prophets Chapter 17. (n.d.). Verse 51.

The prophets I Chapter 17 Verse 51-56. (n.d.).

turkeytravelcentre. (2022). The Cave of Abraham. *Turkey travel blog*, 1.

Văduva, S. (2016). *From corruption to modernity the evoluation of Romania's entrepreneurship culture.* New York Dordrecht London: Springer Cham Heidelberg .

Milton Keynes UK
Ingram Content Group UK Ltd.
UKHW050656280324
440307UK00012B/429

9 781917 185967